MW00523145

Valencia

City of Fire

susaeta

Palau de la Música i Congressos is an avant-garde design building inaugurated in 1987, prefiguring the cosmopolitan, learned and dynamic character of Valencian society.

Edited by:
Thema, Equipo Editorial, S.A.

Photography by:
Frederic Camallonga
Fotografía Astillero (pages 18-19)

Translated by:
Carole Patton

© SUSAETA EDICIONES S.A.
Campezo s/n – 28022 Madrid (Spain)
Tel: 913 009 100 – Fax: 913 009 118

Torres de Serranos is a monumental Gothic gateway which was added to the city walls as a triumphal arch at the end of the 14th century.

Contents

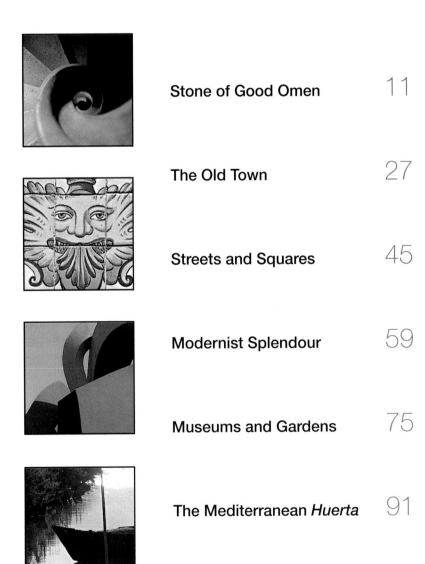

Valencia

City of Fire

Beautiful eyes look everywhere:
They can see how the City of Valencia stretches before them, and,
on the other side, the sea; they can see the rich and fertile huerta,
And all the other admirable things. And they raise their hands,
To thank God for so many riches.

Poem of The Cid

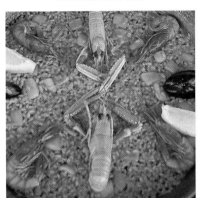

History

The contours of the bell tower are a synthesis of the fighting and religious spirit of the Christians.

Ascent

The inner staircase of the tower goes round and round like a vertical whirlwind of the spirit.

Senses

The fruits of the land and the sea meet at the hearth for the pleasure of our senses.

Homage

The hero who has been paralysed in history is unaware of the passing of the years and the homage being paid by city fauna.

Geometry

The lines traced by the metal structure seem to draw figures in space.

Tradition

The light shining on the young faces of girls dressed in tradional *Falla* costumes evoke the pagan tradition of fire.

L'Umbracle is one of the most spectacular areas of the City of the Arts and Sciences, where the work of man and nature harmonise.

The architectonic harmony of the streets
converging in the triangular-shaped
Plaza del Ayuntamiento.

Valencia

City of Fire

STONE OF GOOD OMEN
Valentia, "the beautiful"

Surrounded by the so-called *Huerta*, (the rich, fertile fields) irrigated by the calm waters of the River Turia which flows into the Mediterranean Sea, Valencia appears as a modern and lively city. Its future is built on ancient traditions which have been formed over thousands of years by different cultures, and which have left a deep mark on the well-disposed and open people of Valencia. The flames of their *fogueres* (bonfires) seem to bring the faces of primitive Iberian inhabitants out of the shadows of the past.

Greek merchants landed on these shores to trade with them, but, according to the historian Titus Livius, it was the Roman consul in Hispania, Junius Bru-

Local Colour and Souvenirs

In the Central Market we can find stalls like the one in the photograph with souvenirs selling paella pans, some of which will be bought as cooking utensils and others as souvenirs.

Convent of Santo Domingo

The cloister with its lovely patio is one of the few vestiges of this Gothic convent built soon after the conquest of Valencia by the Catalano-Aragonese King Jaume I.

Vision of the Past
A bird's-eye view of the rooftops of the *Santos Juanes Church* and the Central Market, examples of two different of styles and public functions.

tus, who founded the town, in 137 BC, as a settlement for the pardoned troops of the Lusitanian Viriato. Brutus called it *Valentia*, meaning in Latin "good omen", "strength" and "might". Seventy years or so later, the town had become the capital of *Valentia Edentanorum* and one of the most important capitals on the Hispano-Mediterranean coast. There are signs that, in order to make the most of the water coming from the nearest mountains and the fertile surrounding land, the Romans carried out important irrigation works. And so, this is how the Valencian *Huerta* began to get its reputation.

The Market-Garden City of the Moors

After the period of Visigothic domination, the city fell into the hands of the Moors in 718, who turned it into a splendid market-garden city. It is said that Al-Hakam II, the caliph of Córdoba, ordered an advanced and complex system of irrigation to be constructed for the benefit of

Estación del Norte

A magnificent example of Modernist architecture and the birth of an age marked by the development of overland transport, of which the railway was the first and mightiest locomotive of progress.

the farmers, as well as the creation of the oldest Tribunal in Europe, the *Tribunal de las Aguas* ("The Water Council"), whose members still meet every Thursday, dressed in their special black overalls, in front of the Cathedral door known as *Puerta de los Apóstoles*, to deal with matters concerning the use of water and settle disputes regarding irrigation. The procedure is completely verbal and the decision of the syndics is final. The period of Arab domination was an age of prosperity, growing orange and mulberry trees and rice, and carrying out arts and crafts such as ceramics, paper making, weaving, silk etc. In 1092, after the murder of the Moorish king, Al-Qadir, Rodrigo Díaz de Vivar (The Cid) governed the city until his death in 1099, and his widow, Doña Jimena, continued to do so until 1102. It was during the battles of the Valencia campaign when the Cid killed "Búcar, that king from beyond the seas, I won the sword, Tizona, worth one thousand golden marks", as it is sung in the famous *Cantar de Mio Cid* (Poem of The Cid). But The Cid's dominion was a short-lived one, and the Almorávides conquered it once more, this time for 136 years.

Medieval Splendour of Valencia

Jaume I of Aragón entered Valencia on 9th October, 1238, the Day of Saint Dionysus, which is why this is the date of the Feast of the Region of Valencia. It is popularly known as the *Mocaorà*, because it is the custom for men to give women *piuletes* and *tronadors*, delicious marzipan sweets, wrapped up in beautiful silk handkerchiefs (*mocadors*).

With the swearing in of the Valencian code of laws and customs in 1261, Jaume I proclaimed the self-government of the Kingdom of Valencia. The houses and farmsteads taken from the Moors were given to Christian priests, to the middle-class and to the common people. Knight-Crusaders, who had been displeased with the fact that the king had not allowed the sacking of the city, also received their share. The following year, the monarch ordered the Cathedral to be built, where what is supposedly the mythical Holy Grail is kept, something for which so many Knights of the Round Table fought so hard.

During the Middle Ages, Pedro IV *el Ceremonioso* did much to embellish the city and ordered a new wall to be built. He did so after the Valencians held the

Ayuntamiento (City Hall)

The dark lion, proud and alert, watches over the city hall from amidst the domes, with its mane being caressed by the Mediterranean breeze.

Bullring

The *Plaza de Toros* of Valencia is one of the most important bullrings in Spain. Aficionados and tourists alike come here to witness the ritual sacrifice of the bull.

Santos Juanes Church
Imposing 17th –century church, a fine example of that style representing the expression of grandeur and power and known as Baroque.

A View of Valencia
Seen from the *Torres de Serranos*, the city rooftops stretch before our eyes, interrupted every now and again by historical towers such as that of the *Micalet*.

so-called War of the Union in 1348. At the end of the same century, religious intolerance led to a massacre of Jews. As well as all this, dynastic disputes between the Count of Urgel and Fernando de Antequera encouraged the so-called *bandos de Valencia*, whose bloody clashes marked the second decade of the 15th century. However, the *quattrocento valenciano* was one of the most splendorous moments in the history of the city until the bloody struggle between the masses and the nobility known as the *Guerra de Germanía* from 1519 to 1522.

The Golden Age

It is said that the 15th and 16th centuries were Valencia's "Golden Age", as a great development took place in all social and economic aspects, turning Valencia into one of the most important Mediterranean cities. Its powerful merchants managed to achieve intense trade through the port, especially in agricultural products and a growing ceramic and silk industry. This is why the Catholic Monarchs ordered the construction of the *Llotja dels Mercaders* (Commodity Exchange), also known as the *Llotja de la Seda* (Silk Exchange), due to the volume of industry and trade being carried out. It was in this impressive Gothic building that Felipe II's wedding

Grand Finale

On the night of the Feast of St. Joseph, the 19th of March, one by one, the *fallas* (figures made from papier-mâché and cardboard) are set on fire amid the noise and flashes of fireworks, and the atavistic fascination of those who are present.

The Fallera's Offering

Dressed up in typical regional costume, the *fallera* (Queen of the *Fallas*) takes her floral offering to the patroness of the city, *Mare de Déu dels Desamparats* ("Our Lady of the Forsaken"), followed by fellow townspeople who seem to emerge from the shadows of time.

was celebrated. Aside from its mercantile industry, there was also a feverish literary production with names such as Joanot Martorell, the author of *Tirant lo Blanc* ("The White Knight") the famous book of knight-errantry mentioned in Cervante's *Don Quixote de la Mancha*, when the priest is examining the books in Don Quixote's house: *"My God!",* *exclaimed the priest out loud, "here* *is Tirant lo Blanc, the famous book* *of chivalry! Give me it, I must admit* *that I have found in it great satis-* *faction and amusement."* A contemporary of Joanot Martorell was Ausiàs March, one of the greatest poets in the Valen-

cian language, and who introduced some of the essential elements of modern poetry, such as day-to-day reality, and the description of the great changes that were taking place in society due to the transit from the Middle Ages to the Renaissance:

"Let the masses hold joyful festivi- *ties, in praise of God, with great* *entertainment; and let delightful* *orchards, squares and streets be* *scenarios of chansons de geste..."*

Together with these artists, we must also mention the famous doctor and theologian, Arnau de Vilanova, whose ideas caused the

clergy, and even the Pope in Rome, many a headache, as well as the humanist and philosopher, Juan Luis Vives, whose ideas led him to taking refuge in Bruges, where he would live for the rest of his days, far from the persecution of the Spanish inquisition. One of the most important events in the cultural history of Spain took place in Valencia in 1475. It was the printing of the first incunabulum in Spain, the *Comprehensorium* of John the Grammarian, whose date has been documentarily proved. However, it is believed, and historically accepted, that the first Spanish printing press of

movable type invented by Gutenberg was set up in Valencia a few years earlier, and that, before the date the *Comprehensorium* was published, other works had already been printed: for example, *Ethica* and *Politica* by Aristotle, as well as *Obres y trobes en lahor de la Verge Maria*, which included compositions in Castilian and Valencian presented at the first poetry competition held in honour of the Virgin, in Valencia. Therefore, with this solid cultural background, it is not surprising that, centuries later, Valencian authors who were contemporary to Lope de Vega founded the well-known *Academia de los Nocturnos*, to which Guillén de Castro belonged, famous for being the author of *Las Mocedades del Cid*, a play that inspired Corneille's *Le Cid*.

The Fire of San José

It is said that the primitive Iberian rite of the fire was assimilated by Christian liturgy on special dates. The *fallas*, also called *fogueres* by the Valencians, which are lit for the *Día de San José* [Feast of St. Joseph, 19th March] are also of pagan origin. It is also said that this custom dates back to the Middle Ages, since St Joseph is the patron saint of carpenters. Supposedly, after the troops of Jaume I *el Conquistador* ("The Conqueror") had entered the city, there was a boom in all sectors, meaning that many guilds were forced to work even when it was dark, to the light of oil-lamps. Carpenters were amongst those affected, and would hang their oil-lamps on a special apparatus called *pelmodo*, *estai*, *parot* or *pagès*, which was a kind of tall, straight, stand with various branches from where they would hang their lamps.

On the arrival of spring, precisely coinciding with the Feast

The Day of the Fallas
In the warm spring Mediterranean sunshine, *falleras* proudly stroll along the street, showing off their delicate costumes and headdresses.
Museo Fallero
A curious museum where posters, leaflets, magazines and other documents related with the *fallas* can be seen, together with the original *ninots* (figures) that have been spared from the flames.

of Saint Joseph, as the days were longer and artificial light was no longer necessary, the carpenters would have a good clean-out and get rid of all unnecessary items, including the *pelmodos*. Therefore, the *fusters* would put them out on the street and the district known as *El Carmen* would be filled with *pelmodos*, which would all end up getting burnt.

Over the years, carpenters would take advantage of this situation and, along with the burning of their *pelmodos*, they would get rid of other useless items lying around in their workshops or houses. It probably occurred to somebody one day to "dress" a *pelmodo*, making it look like a grotesque figurine , which led to deliberately designing figures specifically for this purpose, with satirical notes or other elements expressing mockery, mordacity or criticism. These figures eventually became

known as *ninots*, the name given to the figures that would end up being burnt.

All the *ninots* make up the *falla*, which is a critical or humoristic expression made by their creators of certain, everyday, popular subjects regarding political, economical or social etc. matters. The *fallas*, which are made of papier-mâché, wood and other highly-combustible materials, can be huge in size and are "planted" on the streets during the week of the Fallas, being burnt on the night of Saint Joseph.

Throughout the whole week, many "ritual ceremonies" are held, which are characterised by the continuous explosion, banging and cracking of all kinds of fireworks and firecrackers, known as *traques* and *mascletades*, both by day and by night. On the night of the *cremà*, the grand finale, the reddish glow caused by the

flames of the *fogueres* (bonfires), along with the tremendous noise and flashing of fireworks, make it look as if the entire city of Valencia were on fire. All the *ninots* are burnt, except the one that has been "pardoned" by popular vote, on that magical night which announces the arrival of spring.

Over the years, the *fallas* have gradually grown in size and complexity, and now they are made and assembled in huge warehouses located on an industrial estate known as *Ciudad del artista fallero* ("City of the *Falla* Artist").

During the mid-nineteenth century, the first *llibrets de falla* appeared, booklets through which poetasters would compete for prizes with their satirical verses. Shortly after this, magazines and leaflets were published which would indicate where the *fallas* were, the in-

Nymph and Dove
Much to the surprise of the dove, a beautiful nymph emerges from the waters of the fountain of the *Plaza de la Virgen*.

The Power of the Flames
On the night of the *cremà* (burning) all the figures are devastated by the flames, the Valencians acknowledging their purifying effect.

tentions of their creators and any anecdote concerning their making. One of the most famous magazines on *fallas* was *Pensat i fet*, which first appeared in 1912 and, apart from the years of the Spanish Civil War, was published successively every year until 1972.

The celebration of the *Fallas* in Valencia includes dancing on the streets or in the *Casal Fallero*, as well as the colourful parade of girls and women dressed in typical costume, taking their floral offering to the chapel of the patroness of the city, the *Mare de Déu dels Desamparats* (Our Lady of the Forsaken), at whose feet an incredible carpet of flowers is soon formed. These flowers are used to make a tapestry of the image of the *Mare de Déu*.

Paella For Special Occasions

The celebration of the *Fallas* is one of the most famous in Spain, and these festivities would not be complete without the presence of a *buñolería* (pastry seller) near each *falla*. Valencians have also been well-inclined to connect celebrating with eating. One of the most typical dishes for special occasions has always been *paella*, that exquisite and tasty rice dish. For centuries, the Moors acclimatised rice-growing to Valencian fields. In 1238, when Jaume I *el Conquistador* conquered the city, the rice paddies almost reached the city gates. In order to avoid epidemics of malaria, the king limited the growing of rice to the areas near *La Albufera*, where there were also abun-

dant eels. Some experts believe that this was one of the first types of fish to be eaten with rice, cooked, seasoned and served in a round, shallow, metallic dish which Castilians called a *paila* and Valencians, a *paella*.

Due to the versatility of rice, it can be prepared in many ways and with many different ingredients, giving rise to dishes such as *paella marinera*, *arròs a banda*, etc. delicately seasoned with rosemary and saffron, in accordance with Arab taste. Seemingly, it was due to the synthesis or combination of these dishes that a special one was created that took the name of the pan or dish in which it was cooked: *paella*.

Typical Valencian paella is rice cooked with chicken or rabbit, various kinds of green beans

and butter beans and, when in season, snails. However, these are the basic ingredients, which can be added to or modified depending on the circumstances and products available in the region, which is why it is usual to find fish and shellfish in *paellas*, especially in restaurants along the coast. In any case, *paella* has gone from being something only eaten on a special occasion in the region of Valencia, to being one of, if not *the*, most representative Spanish dish on an international scale.

The *Huerta* of Valencia is also famous for its orange groves and its sedge plantations, a rushlike plant whose tuberous fruits are used to make the typical and extremely popular drink known as *horchata*. Especially during the summer, cafe-terias and *horchaterías* sell this cool, refreshing, sweet drink that looks like milk and which can be drunk on its own or accompanied by *fartons* (a kind of sweet breadsticks) or *rosquilletas* (a type of crunchy biscuit). Well-famed in Valencia is the old *Horchatería Santa Catalina*, beside the *Plaza de la Virgen*, to where *horchata*-lovers flock from all over Spain and Europe.

The City of the Future

Well-established on solid traditions, Valencia looks towards the 21st century as a cosmopolitan city ready to face the challenges of the future. Magnificent examples of this dynamic horizon are the modern buildings of the *Palau de la Música* and the *Instituto Valenciano de Arte Moderno* (IVAM), whose *Centro Julio González* is dedicated to the works of the father of twentieth-century Spanish sculpture and to those of the painter Ignacio Pinazo, one of the most representative Valencian artists of the nineteenth century. However, the most audacious and imaginative works of modern Valencia is the complex of the *Ciutat de les Arts i de les Ciències*, consisting of the *Palau de les Arts*, *L'Hemisfèric*, *L'Umbracle*, *L'Oceanogràfic* and the *Museu de les Ciències*.

And so, Valencia, also known as the "city of the flowers", stands facing the Mediterranean Sea, on the banks of the River Turia and built on the foundations of genuine tradition, with the healthy ambition of holding a relevant position along with other great Mediterranean cities.

La Albufera

This "small sea", its meaning in Arabic, determines the landscape and agricultural wealth of Valencia. It is also the natural background of the novels by the popular Spanish author, Vicente Blasco Ibáñez.

The Old Town

Mercantile Nobility. Once Valencia had been conquered by King Jaume I, farmers, artisans and merchants were the artificers of a prosperous mercantile industry. The dynamic role played by the mercantile bourgeoisie led the Catholic Monarchs to ordering the construction of the *Llotja dels Mercaders* (Commodity Exchange). The building, a superb example of flamboyant Gothic, was designed by the architect Pere Compte and the upper floor contained the *Consolat de Mar*.

Sala de contrataciones ("The Transactions' Hall"). The importance of the trade that was carried out in the *Llotja dels Mercaders* led to the construction of a large, refined hypostyle hall, whose tall, helicoidal columns support the high stellar vaults, whilst daylight filters through the stained-glass windows, thus creating the ambience of a cathedral.

Spiral Staircase. The form of the spiral staircase arouses in us a peculiar sensation, as if it had been created by the frenzy of the transactions taking place in this building.

The Old Town

Financial Fortress. The row of windows, the battlements and the square tower crown the façade of the *Llotja dels Mercaders*, which was also known as the *Llotja de la Seda* (The Silk Exchange).

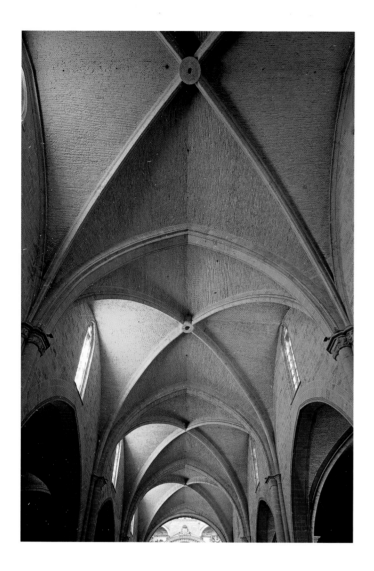

The Old Town

Plant Motifs. The ogives over the central nave of Valencia Cathedral are like an imaginary geometric tree, whose angles are projections of light streaming through the tall windows.

The Cathedral Dome. The ribbed vaults and windows in the Cathedral, a synthesis of the Gothic and *Mudéjar* styles, reflect the transcendental meaning of the Christian spirit and faith that inspired the Reconquest.

Bell Tower. Seen from the *Plaza de l'Almoina*, we have an interesting perspective of *El Micalet*, the name given by the inhabitants of the city to the bell tower of the Cathedral that was the Gothic symbol of the Kingdom of Valencia.

The Old Town

El Micalet by Day and by Night. The 14th – century octagonal bell tower is 68 metres tall and is known as *El Micalet*, *Miquelet* or *Miguelete* (different ways of saying the name *Miguel*, "Michael" in Spanish), as it was blessed on the Day of Saint Michael.

El Micalet and the Puerta de los Hierros. Twelve bells playing the seven tones and semitones of the scale seem as if they mould the Baroque lines on the main door of the temple.

Torres de Serranos. The rear façade of the gate tower reveals the sober, precise lines of late 14th – century military Gothic architecture. Built on the old city walls, its monumentality seems to exalt the triumph of Christian knights.

Fortress and Bridge. *Puerta de Serranos*, built by Pere Balaguer, was part of the city fortifications when the Christian kingdoms fought against the Arabs or against each other. The bridge over the River Turia was added later.

Stone and Monster. Detail of one of the Gothic arches of the rear of *Torres de Serranos*, presided over by one of the many gargoyles adorning it.

Symmetry and Battlements. The steps on the rear part of *Torres de Serranos* lead up to the parapet walk, like a symmetrical ornamental border on the wall. Visitors come and go as if they were ancient Christian warriors.

The Old Town

The Old Town

Santos Juanes. This magnificent 17th –century church marked the beginning of Baroque architecture in the urban landscape of Valencia. The façade is adorned with stone sculptures and a retable, work of the master sculptor Jacobo Bartessi.

Baroque Splendour. *Santos Juanes* Church is one of the greatest of Valencian Baroque monuments. The ensemble of sculpted stone figures appears like a reference of lines within a framework of a space dedicated to exalting the power of faith.

Torres de Quart. The sturdy and harmonious Valencian Gothic architecture seen here on this 15th – century gate, defines not only a style of architecture, but also the character of its people who wanted to open up to the sea and trade; the landscape of a prosperous Valencia.

High Up On Guard. Valencia has preserved its battlemented defensive walls and gates, from the top of which there is a splendid panoramic view of the sea and surrounding countryside.

Symbol of the Reconquest. Pedro IV *el Ceremonioso* ordered the city defences to be strengthened with high walls containing gates such as the *Puerta de Quart*, which became popularly known as monuments of Christian warriors.

The Old Town

Church of San Martín. 15th – century medieval church whose design and ornamentation exalt the values of the Reconquest. In spite of its loss of walls, we can see fine sculptures by the Flemish school, such as the equestrian statue known as *el cavall de Sant Martí* that symbolically represents Christ as a beggar receiving a piece of the saint's mantle.

The Old Town

Convent of Santo Domingo. Beautiful and original ceiling in the *Capilla de los Reyes* ("Chapel of the Kings") of the *Convento de Santo Domingo*, another example of religious Gothic architecture in Valencia.

Gothic Elegance. The ribbed vault, the tall, slender columns and the tall, narrow stained-glass windows with Gothic arches all create a warm atmosphere in the Chapter House of the medieval Convent of *Santo Domingo*.

Portal de la Mar. Valencia, in the 18th century, was sensitive to the academic spirit and to enhancing the light and sobriety in all its practical and artistic manifestations.

Light and Tranquillity. A splendid fountain stands in the square in front of the *Basílica Mare de Déu dels Desamparats* (The Basilica of Our Lady of the Forsaken), the patroness of the city and where hundreds of flowers are deposited on the Feast of Saint Joseph.

The Old Town

Streets and Squares

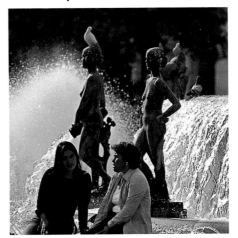

The Triumph of Water. The fountain of the *Plaza de la Virgen*, with its cascades, is like a homage to water, such a vital element for the people of the *Huerta*. The sound of its flowing water is also that of the passing of time and the continuity of life which goes on beyond the historical events and the eternal contradiction of fire. The ever-flowing waters are a delight for passers-by.

Carrer dels Cavallers. Main thoroughfare of the old Gothic quarters, this street still has vestiges of the medieval splendour of Valencia. Its very name ("Knights' Street") comes from the numerous noblemen who came to live here once Jaume I had entered the city.

Paseo de los Nobles. *Carrer dels Cavallers*, which begins on the northern side of the *Palau de la Generalitat*, was where rich merchants and nobles lived. Some of those mansions still survive today in between all kinds of shops, businesses, workshops, restaurants, cafeterias, bars, etc.

Streets and Squares

Palau de la Generalitat. This palace, started in 1482 by Pere Compte, stands at beginning of the *Carrer dels Cavallers*, which used to be the assembly hall of the old *Cortes*, one of whose many functions was to collect "general" tax, and today houses the regional parliament.

Plaza de Manises. Dominating one side of this old public space is the 16th – century Baylía Palace, which takes its name from the fact that it used to be the residence of the *Baile General*, the Public Treasury magistrate. The only remaining vestiges of the original Gothic design can be found in the austere inner courtyard, the rest of the building having suffered many reforms over the centuries.

Streets and Squares

Streets and Squares

Heart of the Old Quarters. The *Plaza de Manises* was the centre of commerce during the city's period of medieval splendour.

Shadows and Stones seem to hold a dialogue on *Calle del Convent de la Puridad*, a dearly loved spot in the old town, whilst the silhouette of a passer-by is a living reminiscence of time which has come to a standstill.

Plaça Rodona. A popular area where the cries of the sellers of the street market mingle with the murmur of shoppers, tourists or onlookers, amid trees, plants, bars, cafeterias, restaurants and taverns, resulting in a lively atmosphere characteristic of an open city.

Streets and Squares

Plaça Rodona. A pigeon takes off from the fountain with four spouts and crowned by a light, in the middle of the square, looking as if it wished to draw the invisible line of its circumference.

Streets and Squares

Carrer de la Pau. During the 19th century, the urban landscape of Valencia experienced a great transformation. A result of the latter are, for example, the streets called *La Pau and Pintor Sorolla*, a prolongation of *Calle de las Barcas*.

Modernity. The second Development Plan meant the boom of the Modernist movement, whose aesthetics determined the city's new look. Tall buildings arose, decorated with floral motifs, wrought iron and stained glass.

Plaza de la Reina. The elaborately-worked domes of Modernist buildings rival in beauty with the austere architectonic lines of the Church of *San Martín's* bell tower.

Nightlife. The *Plaza de Tossal* is just one of the favourite rendezvous spots of the Valencians, open people who are very fond of their leisure time.

Open At Dawn. *Sant Jaume* is a typical bar in the district of *El Carmen* which is open until its last patron is finally overcome by sleep.

Night Road. When the sun has set, the Gothic street of *Carrer dels Cavallers* is transformed with the opening of bars and filled with the sound of laughter.

Whispers. Friendly, easy-going people, many Valencians gather at the counter just for the sake of killing time and chatting.

Streets and Squares

The Dawn of a New Age

City Hall. The imposing building of the City Council is a symbol of the city planning carried out during the second half of the 19th century. This was when the former site of the Convent of *San Francisco* was replaced by the triangular *Plaza del Caudillo, del País Valenciano*, later known as the *Plaza del País Valencià* and today as the *Plaza del Ayuntamiento*, completely transforming the look of the area.

Dynamism. The prosperity and power of Valencia can be appreciated (left) by the conception of its architecture and its fondness of water, maybe inherited from the Moors, as a symbol of life.

Modernity. From 1887, the Modernist movement profoundly influenced the city development.

The Dawn of a New Age

Neuralgic Point. The *Plaza del Ayuntamiento* (below) is the result of the first city Development Plan.

Palacio del Marqués de Dos Aguas. An emblematic Baroque building designed by Hipólito Rovira. Its façade full of windows and balconies are a fine example of Spanish Rococo at its best.

Exquisite Architecture. Superb detail on the *Palacio del Marqués de Dos Aguas*, a masterpiece of Valencian Baroque, which today houses the National Ceramic Museum.

A Detail. The façade of the *Palacio del Marqués de Dos Aguas* is by Ignacio Vergara, who is said to have materialised his own delirium in this alabaster ornamentation. Luis Domingo also contributed to the magnificent ensemble with his provocative sculptures.

The Dawn
of a New Age

The Dawn of a New Age

Colegio del Patriarca or del Corpus Christi. In this beautiful Renaissance patio, the statue of the viceroy, archbishop and patriarch, and later saint, Juan de Ribera, is maybe meditating on the idea of perfection bequeathed by the Romans and Greeks.

The Greco-Roman Renaissance.
The ensemble of the college and
church of the Patriarch or Corpus
Christi represents the triumph of
Humanism regarding the concept
of space. Inside, paintings by Juan
de Juanes, Francisco Ribalta and
Luis de Morales can be admired.

Dome of Light. Beautiful stained-glass windows lighten the vault covering the Chapter House of the Convent of *Santo Domingo*.

Wrought Iron, Glass and Tiles. The Central Market is a masterpiece of Modernist civil architecture. Its 8,000 m2 make it one of the largest markets on the Continent and its architectural beauty a true cathedral to food.

The Dawn of a New Age

Stained Glass in the Market. Modernism gave great importance to design and ornamentation as well as the overall use of materials such as wrought iron and glass, a style which, here in the *Mercado Central*, served as a vehicle for the architectural exaltation of the Valencians' hedonistic spirit and their love of produce from the land and sea.

The Symbol of the Country. The stained-glass windows show details and scenes which celebrate the agricultural riches of the irrigated and cultivated plain *(huerta)* of Valencia or reproduce the symbols of Valencian identity. Every morning, the nearly 1000 stalls of the market produce an incredible explosion of colours and aromas.

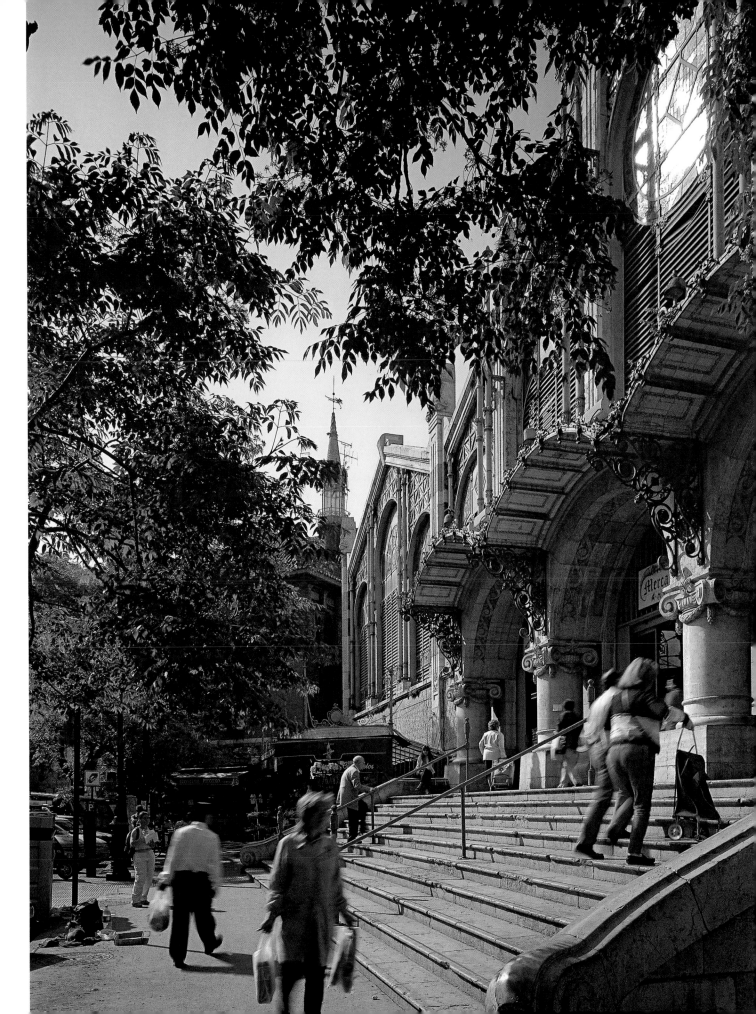

Estación del Norte. The arrival of the railway in the 19th century was the symbol of progress and modernity, and railway stations, such as this one at Valencia, were the expression of an architecture that artistically satisfied the desires of the industrial society.

Ornamentation. The column, covered with multicoloured mosaics representing scenes of the *huerta*, enhances the spherical lamps which hang from it in the station foyer. The railway brought airs of progress to Valencia.

A Leap into the Future. The organisation of underground transport and the need to construct new, modern stations, such as this one of *La Alameda*, are one of the clearest examples of the dynamism of a city wishing to occupy a privileged position in the Mediterranean basin. Nowadays, Valencia is a thriving agricultural, industrial and manufacturing area, particularly of ceramics.

The Dawn of a New Age

Area of Expansion. *Calle de las Barcas* was opened up from the *Plaza del Ayuntamiento* with the purpose of making a tree-lined avenue.

The Dawn of a New Age

Financial Centre. At the end of *Calle de las Barcas*, the monumental building of the *Banco de Valencia* appears like the prow of an ocean liner.

Calatrava Bridge. Modern and futuristic, this viaduct boldly displays its radiated arch as if it were an architectural reflection of water hung in mid air. It is a new way of conceiving the urban landscape and its means of communication.

Futuristic Viaduct. The Valencian architect, Santiago Calatrava, designs bridges as cultural phenomena. Their concrete structures and beams are cast into space evoking subtle Gothic forms that seem to emerge from consciousness and the subconscious.

The Dawn of a New Age

Museums and Gardens

The Culture of Public Spaces.
Valencia is a city which has inherited the Arabs' fondness for gardens and parks as well as their love of knowledge. The modern structures of the *Museu de les Ciències* (Science Museum) are a splendid synthesis of a cultural history which has kept on advancing in its humanistic, scientific and technological development since it first started to do so centuries ago. This museum invites us all to live an exciting adventure.

A Background of Learning. This detail of the helicoidal structure of DNA is just one example of the way of displaying scientific discoveries which have been essential to mankind and gives us an idea of how didactic the Valencia Science Museum is.

Museums and Gardens

Foucault Pendulum. The oscillation of the pendulum with a minimum friction with the air allows hundreds of visitors to see the rotation of the Earth every day, following the experiment of the French physicist Jean Bernard Léon Foucault.

Museums and Gardens

A Game of Shapes. The building of the *Museu de les Ciències*, with its audacious masts and spars made of concrete and glass, looks like something from outer space, a huge construction that looms up in space and on the planetary horizon.

Ciudat de les Artes i de les Ciències. A modern complex whose avant-garde forms and content lead Valencia into a future marked by science and technology and which provides its visitors with a good way of becoming familiar with them.

Spectacular View. The audacious and imposing structures of the buildings comprising the *Museu de les Ciències* and *de L'Hemisfèric* are even more spectacular when lit up at night, making us feel that we are in an age that has not yet come.

Museums and Gardens

A Peaceful Stroll. The Botanical Gardens of Valencia, founded by the naturalist Antonio José Cavanilles at the beginning of the 19th century, were the first of their kind to be created in Spain.

Recreation of the Tropics. Many exotic plants create an atmosphere of being on an adventure in a tropical jungle.

Palm Trees and Ferns. The exuberance of vegetation belonging to other latitudes is possible thanks to the hothouse of the old Botanical Gardens.

Museums and Gardens

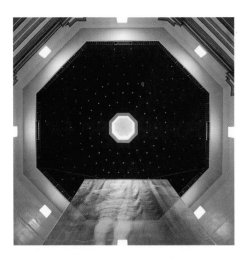

Fine Arts Museum. This detail in the foyer suggests an artistic abstraction in which a dark monolith is illuminated from high up in space.

Garden of Creation. Behind the beautiful patio and gardens, we can find one of the most complete and interesting picture galleries in Spain.

The Dome of the Spirit. The Seminary and Convent of *San Pío V*, which today houses the Museum of Fine Arts, is a master-piece by Juan Bautista Pérez Castiel, known as the father of Valencian Baroque.

Museums and Gardens

Museums and Gardens

Centre of Avant-Garde Art. The *IVAM* (*Instituto Valenciano de Arte Moderno*) occupies a futuristic building by Carlos Salavadores and an old 13th –century Carmelite convent.

The Antechamber of Vanguardism. The rooms of the *IVAM* house works by magnificent contemporary artists such as the sculptor Julio González.

Matter and Space. Simple lines go from the real to the imaginary in the works of the North American sculptor Tony Smith, which can be seen in the *IVAM*.

Gulliver in the River Turia. The popular character created by the English author, Jonathan Swift, chose the gardens covering the old riverbed as an adventure playground for children.

A World of Fantasy. Gulliver, sometimes a giant and others a dwarf, carries the children to a world of fantasy, making them go down slides, steps and curious passageways.

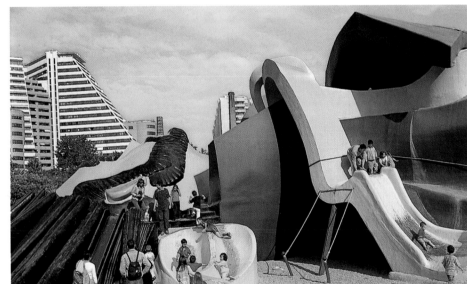

Giants and Lilliputians. Gulliver's Park, in the Turia Gardens, is a delight for children who become immersed in a fabulous world of make believe.

Puente del Mar. An 18th - century bridge which is a Renaissance masterpiece. Its solid stone structure elegantly spans the Turia riverbed, whose dark waters calmly flow in accordance with the passing of time, just like in the image of the Greek philosopher, Heraclitus.

Museums and Gardens

Puente del Real. In the Turia Gardens only the bridges evoke the old riverbed on its way through Valencia. Today, no longer do waters pass through the stone arches of the old bridges, but bicycles.

The Mediterranean *Huerta*

The Lake of Life. The Moors called this mirror of freshwater south of Valencia *albufera*, meaning "little sea". Many species of fish can be found here and it is the natural habitat of migratory and sea birds; it is also the ideal land for rice-growing, for which Valencia is so renowned, and has been the source of inspiration for the writer Blasco Ibáñez, who set his novels *La Barraca* and *Cañas y Barro* amidst the salt marshes and rushes of the area.

Promenade. More than two kilometres of promenade border the old districts of *El Cabañal* and *La Malvarrosa*, where locals and visitors walk along in the Mediterranean sunshine, taking in the salt sea breeze.

Families, Couples and Bathers. Locals and visitors strolling along the wide promenade at *La Malvarrosa*, breathing in the sea air and enjoying the beauty of the Mediterranean sunlight that the Valencian artist Joaquín Sorolla knew how to portray so well in his paintings.

The Mediterranean

Paella a la Malvarrosa. The typical dish of Valencia and the symbol of Spanish cooking is, without any doubt, the paella, an exaltation of the five senses, which are all interconnected, one arousing the other at the sight and smell of this dish.

Beside the Sea. Whilst some go for a stroll along the beach, others enjoy their *paella marinera* and *sangría*. And so, time passes between the coming and going of the waves and the laughter of those who enjoy being in one of the most modern cities on the Levant.

Huerta

Salt Marshes. The rice paddies that surround *La Albufera* of Valencia produce the third part of Spanish rice.

Boats. Small boats belonging to the fishermen of *La Albufera* in *Catarroja* harbour, separated from the sea by *La Dehesa*.

Between the River and the Sea. *La Albufera* is fed by the River Turia and is communicated with the sea through three canals, one of them being known as *El Palmar*.

The Mediterranean Huerta

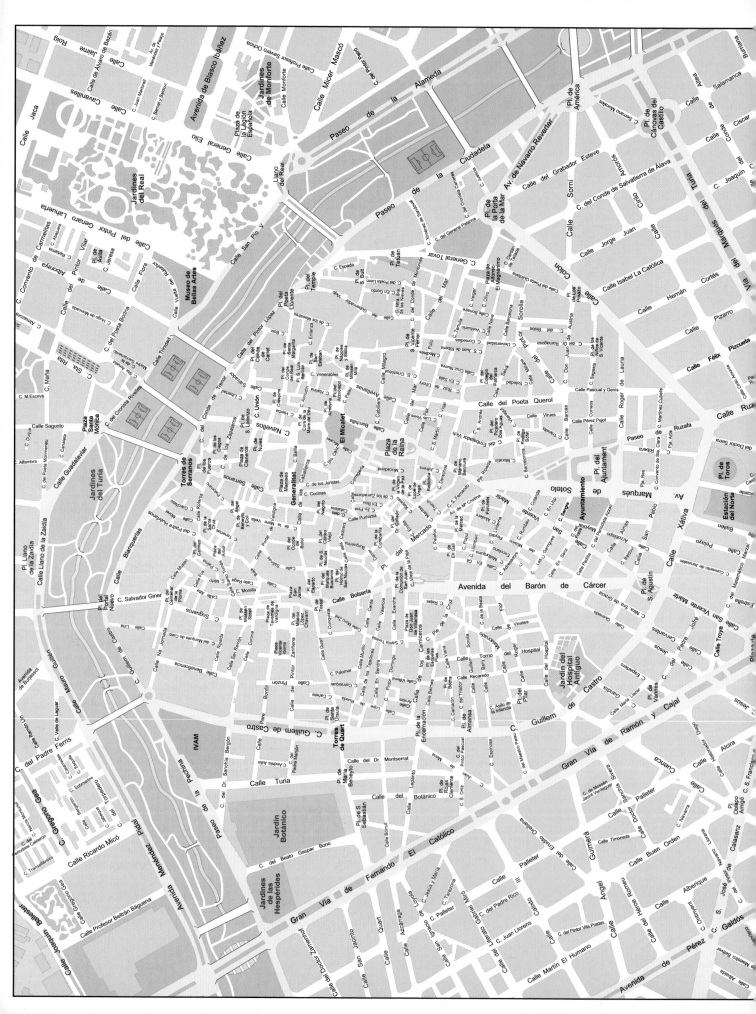